Bull Days

Tina Giannoukos was born in Melbourne. As a child, she lived for several years in Greece, where she completed her primary-school education. She holds a PhD in creative writing from the University of Melbourne, has worked in teaching, journalism and law, and has held a Varuna Fellowship for New Writers. Tina has also lived and worked in Beijing, and has travelled widely, including in Egypt. She has read her poetry in Greece and China. Her first collection of poetry, *In a Bigger City*, was published in 2005.

Also by Tina Giannoukos

In a Bigger City (2005)

BULL DAYS

Tina Giannoukos

ARCADIA

First published 2016 by ARCADIA
the general books imprint of
Australian Scholarly Publishing Pty Ltd

7 Lt Lothian St North, North Melbourne 3051
tel: 03 9329 6963 / *fax:* 03 9329 5452
aspic@ozemail.com.au / www.scholarly.info

ISBN: 978-1-925333-62-6

To my parents Athanasios & Athanasia Giannoukos

Contents

Acknowledgements

Poems from this collection have appeared, some in slightly different form, in *Antipodes: Literary and Educational Periodical of the Greek-Australian Cultural League of Melbourne*, *Blast: Poetry and other Critical Writing*, and *New Antigone*; Kris Hemensley's blog *poetry & ideas*; in the anthologies *Southern Sun, Aegean Light: Poetry of Second-Generation Greek-Australians* (ed. N.N. Trakakis, Arcadia, 2011) and *The Attitude of Cups: An Anthology of Australian Poetry about Tea, Wine and Coffee* (ed. Sue Stanford, Melbourne Poets Union with the assistance of Rebus Press, 2011); and in *Border-Crossings: Narrative and Demarcation in Postcolonial Literatures and Media* (eds Russell West-Pavlov, Justus Makokha and Jennifer Wawrzinek, Winter, 2012).

I am grateful to Alex Skovron, Mal McKimmie, Kris Hemensley, Marion May Campbell, Ron Pretty, Arthur Andronas and Jenny Lee; and to Nick Walker of Australian Scholarly Publishing.

I

When the time comes, whenever that be,
I shall look back to my ancestors,
seafarers all, gliding over oceans,
now coming into ports. This earth,
this blue planet, will not circumscribe me.
I will sail across the empty doom searching
for cyclopean marvels; a half-horse, half-man
figure will appear from behind that band
of stars beyond the edge of the Milky Way.
The astrophysics of our encounter,
this dark energy of love, are unknown.
In a singular moment the explosion
that drove all things apart drove us too.
In space I hold the horn of plenty.

II

When you touch me it is the hand of God.
I agree to restrain the gravity of this emotion.
I begin the long march in death's dominion.
I bear imperfectly the thought that I'm alone.

Mona Lisa's smile remains enigmatic.
This is the only wisdom I possess:
They marked you. They marked you all your life.
Moonlight still shines on what you left behind.

The will is muscular. Like muscle, it tears.
You sentence me to hard labour. Once,
I was beautiful but that was rapture.
The tongue of love tastes tough in these bull days.

This is the conspiracy of the figure two:
the flowers in the garden grow mottled.

III

The phone rings. I compose myself,
but breath catches in unrestrained glee.
Am I up for this game of hearts?
It's easy to slip. I'm on my knees.
I cling to summer's glad profusions,
eat the last of the season's peaches,
sure of their sweet reward.
Your voice is cold. Winter is here.
The wind bites, gets into my bones,
pores close to love, ludicrous without you.
I am red-eyed before this farce. Hallelujah!
'Will you talk to me, please? I am alone.'
The theme of our encounter escapes me—
I thought I was your envoy to the gods.

IV

When you strode up, I realised
I'd forgotten your face. You were spot-on
I would deny you even if
I finished each sentence you uttered.
Really, a stroll past the old haunts
would remind you how you needed
to rest from the bareness of me,
and, yes, the daffodils dried again.
It may be that I can't recall
any lover's face post-coitus,
a reason to pardon my fickleness,
though you never stay put.
You keep faith when it matters most.
Take heart, you may forget my name.

V

I scan your face—so effeminate—
for mark of my remembrance.
As I recall it was late summer,
so early to be worrying about us.
I'm shocked to catch the look
that registers but doesn't give
the game away. To know you played
me twice holds the truth I won't
name: it was for zilch. I'm out.
We ordered the banquet, drank wine,
the taste of berries soaked my lips,
stained my breath, mouth on mouth.
The tree outside my window shakes.
My exterior does not allow tears.

VI

you have a lover in every port
I've been loved in every port
the thoughts fly between breaths
I'm not being ironic when I say
no song's been written or poem
that can explain why I don't miss
your touch or breath let's just say
you slit my throat with your kiss
you split my ear with your tongue
my hand coolly slices through vein
red is the colour of my humiliation
next time you'll laugh and I'll blubber
this isn't pretty and I'm not innocent
I'm not responsible for everything

VII

It is impossible to say when
or how, but the crude reluctance
of this encounter to out itself
as the fabrication of two people
in love with hate is typical
of how world affairs proceed—let's say
Salome's tantalising dance, or
an insult at the level of the cell.
I know you are a great man, but why
must I suffer when other men
have offered me the world?
My stars say to find the rhythm
of my breath in the lips that I kiss.
Tonight I kiss the lips of a dead man.

VIII

The silence that haunts the life lived alone
cannot be spoken. On the road the pigeon left to die
pecks at the hand that attempts the rescue. Love,
if it's true love, never dies. Does anyone believe this?
Somewhere a man is dead. Is he grateful? Ask
his soul how he made it through the night
of pain that leached his will. Everything fails
at the crucial moment. O Love! Wet your mouth
on mine. Let me be yours. The heart breaks
in the middle of the night. I pray on my knees.
I wrestle with angels. I am a stranger in my own bed.
I learn that nothing is worth my own death.
I stroll in the garden, the scent of summer strong.
This love is ending. Close my eyes and leave.

IX

On what reading is this failed love based?
The world breathes and I am surprised.
I have no letters, only words on my computer
to tell me you and I made love, were louts.
The cat on the roof opposite my bedroom
stretches, and I think what truth did we draw out?
The voice is seductive, and yours licks
wounds then torments with its silence.
I am in love with your sound, not a man.
Be quick. Flesh is forgotten All skin is soft.
The voice that torments me is the voice of God.
You promised to come, but didn't.
I forgot we'd parted as friends and begged
the gods to flay you alive for your lie.

X

I forget myself, forget I'm yours.
The body trembles in its urgency:
the promise and the vision I drink from.
I forget myself and she knows I will,
knows my hand will glide over flesh
with the urgency of a labour that will undo itself
with the passion of your entry
into this sphere of love and play.
My whisper is overheard, caught
on a breeze that blows itself out
before this heat of summer can undo me.
These breasts are honey to your eyes,
nipples harden as lips close around them.
This is the fire you want, the tremble you seek.

XI

All loves are linked. The liturgy of this affair,
heretical, permits violation. In dialogue,
we discover the monologue. My words
slip between idioms. I am in drag.
The monasticism of your love whets
the tongue, and a startling excessiveness
emerges. You are right to limit
the alphabet of my love. The vowels
of moaning proliferate. Polyphony
disturbs your spare musicality. Bare
is the sound of your pain. No one
can play this harmony of silence and
complaint. My favourite instrument,
right now, is the lyre of lament.

XII

My body shakes off its paralysis.
I don't care if I'm yours.
This is the promise and the vision.
My lover knows resistance.
Her hands glide over flesh.
This dyad cannot last.
I want to bar your entry, my fall
into this sphere of love and flesh.
I bow before this white heat.
Her breasts are honey to my eyes, nipples
harden as lips close around them.
This is the fire I want, the tremble I seek.
It's too late, the time is past for
loving too loose to count as song or praise.

XIII

It's raining outside. All I want is you.
I would tell you that I did not betray you,
but I did abandon you. When I'm seen
for the coward I am, I'll do penance.
Life at the bottom is worse than you think,
all brilliant possibilities, but I merely
tread water. The shadow of the present
is the whip that lashes me in the future.
The final stroke comes when you smile.
I dream of a red sea dyed with my blood.
I will not tell you my name or origin.
Everything recedes from common memory.
I'm fired up, shake out my wet hair. How
can I go back with nothing gained?

XIV

You must sever my aorta,
snap the spinal cord. Be quick.
Make the fans happy. Don't be slow.
They want blood. You know this.
Humour them. This is cowardice,
not tenderness. This is unhelpful.
You know I can gore you.
Don't listen to your critics. Mine
are drinking wine in anticipation.
I'm ready. Your men did their bit.
Now do yours. I hang my head.
My back gleams red. Celebrate
this richness. I'm waiting.
Blood drenches my mouth.

XV

Your hand passes over my body.
'I got it. I got it,' you reiterate,
wishing to dam the cascading deluge
of words, but I'm adrift in the torrent.
An apologia seems hollow juxtaposed
with the laughter of the risked—if only we'd
tethered the weeds along the high road
or planted dandelion in the black ground.
My sublime tears are wasted on this lover—
the mellifluous alphabet of ache
in the afternoon stroll through the gardens
risks the narrowing of the imagination.
In the sculptured stream a dragonfly lays
her eggs while her perfect mate hovers.

XVI

The eruption of this love turns blue. I
saw the crescent moon turn blue. I saw
the half-moon turn blue. I saw two blue moons
in a month. All the moons I saw were blue.
The plumes of ash from the eruption of
your love rose to the top of Earth's hardwired
body. And I saw the moon turn blue
in shame. The ashes of your love bled
into the red sunset I saw in Egypt.
The fire in the forests of your love had
smouldered for years. Blew up into the blaze
the wind fanned from spite. The sun turned blue.
In the smoke-filled sky the sun was indigo.
The moon was blue again that evening.

XVII

In the land of striking women you search
for the one whose spartan body, toned from
the rigours of lovemaking, tresses cut
to the root, yet delicate as a girl
sharpening a knife, will let you grapple
with the image of yourself as the heroic
lover, the man who can win a woman
with the slightest of efforts, let's say, something
resembling the mere exertion of will
before the slight heat of the day, as if
assertion of force might startle the dull
trees or wake the sun from his torpor.
In the pumice after a volcanic eruption
evidence from the magma chamber is sealed.

XVIII

All this politicking. It's a sign. Yeah!
Nothing in it if you're single. Fuck!
Thirty per cent of women live alone. Whoa!
Let's work out a way to tax silence. Cool!
Sixty per cent of men roam the streets. Shit!
No one wants to pair any more. You betcha!
If we put a tax on silence we'll get them. Wow!
It costs money to run silence. Too right!
We can't support these lonely hearts. No!
They have to take responsibility. Absolutely!
Give them subscriptions to porn. Get 'em goin'!
The private is the domain of the public. That's right!
Tell 'em sex is good. Don't panic. It's a ruse!
Is this the Sapphic line? O Sweet! O Love!

XIX

Some nights I smell the sea the oyster smell of brine.
The epic journey begins at the shore of the black sea.
Into the deep seas of hell I pour the libations of sorrow.
The pool of stagnant water at the edge of the world
lies across three mountains I will never scale or see.
The trees silhouetted against the encroaching night
look natural but are full of the menace of ghosts.
A celebration of the day turns into the mournful
note of a cello echoing an ode to a lost opportunity.
This is the last drink before night envelops the epoch
of radical indifference marked by the strict boundary
of reminiscence, yet the coordinates of an unmarked
grief save us the trouble of a headstone or the silly
invocation of mourning to elevate a private injury.

XX

The arena is quiet. The sun is overhead.
Step into the centre. Take your place
among the matadors of the past.
They await your immolation.
Sex is not easy, but it is natural.
I am your bull charging you and you,
a working matador, show your control,
drive the steel into my heart.
When you remove your blackwinged hat,
recall her to whom you dedicate this bull's death.
What trophy to keep? My ears, my tail, my hooves?
No, throw my body parts to your sweetheart.
I hope she hurls flowers at you for it.
The crowd will wave handkerchiefs.

XXI

'At the café? Eat in? Or take-away?'
Oh, that's my lover being open-handed.
That's fine for him. He says it's so passé
the wine-and-dine obsession. I'm branded
complainer, moaner, a real virago.
I yearn for blue chrysanthemums or some
African violets. Purple, please. Macho
blokes wear off when swagger or charms succumb
to daily orthodoxies. For example,
who gets to do the washing up?
Or hosting dinner parties for meddle-
some friends who can't see the poetry. Amen
to that. Let's tow this sinking boat to port
and disembark. 'Oh, you're such a spoilsport.'

XXII

Kneel in the arena and pray I kill you.
Mouth a silent prayer when I charge you.
Now greet me with the best manoeuvres,
let your cape swing in the sun. I said pray.

Watch how I move, and move quietly
into the ring to face me. I will lower
my head for the kill. You have already
wounded me in the shoulder. Up close

you are so nervous, looking over your back.
Your sweetheart is here. She has no idea.
Your moment has come. Aim correctly,
plunge the sword between my shoulder-blades.

Cut your pigtail and retire from the ring.
I am a bull and must die. That is the point.

XXIII

The dark curls, like a rare fringe, are turning grey
but the brown eyes, degenerate, remain. I search for you.
This is my crime: I was never sentimental.
Your face is weathered as the bark on this tree.
These are my dog days. What is the last image of you?
A man pouring wine. You wore the bracelet of
gold and lapis lazuli, like an invitation. In my cement
backyard, a young artist painted the fresco of me bare-breasted.
I searched for your image in the disc before my eyes.
It wasn't some luscious youth I sought, his sensuous fringe
like blond rivers of yearning. I wanted an elaborate dance
of mind, pure spirit, and of a wish for the fall
of your shadow. What does it matter? It is
in contemplation that I know us best.

XXIV

The night casts its blue light. Wraps me in it.
I know the drone of each car that drives past.
The sudden cut of engine leaves no doubt
that someone is being picked up again.
The two next door go off on their evening.
I calculate what conjunction governs
the play between two people who, bent
on love, conjure the sour acrimony
of two wearied by the thing dividing them.
We jumped from kiss to last embrace as if,
fastforwarding, we thought we'd save ourselves
all that trouble down the track. I was not
to know I'd want to make a year of it.
Can I tempt you with the moons of Jupiter?

XXV

my love is one continuous take
no jump-cut no freeze-frame no edit
you capture its image track its
course make it memorable
my love is a reflection on screen
thousands of people are in love today
love is artifice built out of moments
it is an artform like any other
I do not forget you even in sleep
if I want a place in your canon
I must impress with my poetics
the digital long take seems avant-garde
it is the long duration of my love
that breaks with tradition and is radical

XXVI

We played as girls in the carpark
behind the shops. The carpark's no longer
there, as so much from that time isn't.
The girl didn't become a woman.
The woman carries the wound of it.
Somewhere is a grave. She hopes
they've scraped off all the names.
Love blows in like a storm,
stirs up the dirt and grit. It's muck.
The woman knows the articulation:
the heart is a murdering beast and then
the tired references to moon and stars
creep in. The night won't release
its poison quick enough and I'm worn out.

XXVII

You are a slice of my life: we are intimates.
I trace my love for you back ten thousand years
to days of honeycombed rooms and courtyards.
My love for you makes me eternal.

Play and I will be bountiful. I have been before.
But I cannot say I will always be so.
The temperature of your love is changing.
It breaks my heart: there are no words for this.

How do I know? Because you have done this before.
Your love has always been a desert of climatic extremes.
My love for you cannot flourish in this chasm:
ecstatic in its reach it turns scornful in sorrow.

My love becomes extinct. Nothing compares with this.
This rubble of stone is all that remains of its immensity.

XXVIII

I'm alone again at this diversion,
making rhymes that mustn't cross the line
between what's nice and merely crass.
It's a tightrope I'm willing to walk,
though I know the point of tension. Slack,
it's still a noose around my neck.
Bitter recrimination is sour grapes.
I'll drink the glass that's poured. This is heartbreak.
The taste lingers like all good wine, so there's
something to be said for savouring more,
yet I confine myself to one pure swill
of liquid catastrophe. I need an aftertaste,
more character. Wine tastings are ideal
for ditching a lover and getting a new one.

XXIX

Soon, maybe after our next drink, you'll drum
home in that uneven rhythm which I,
for one, perceive to be the usual conundrum
of middle age when, all despondent, the die
cast, men ramble about daughters and a son
intent on crushing all remaining dreams.
You propose instead one more drink, all bon-
homie, Pinot Gris, your pick, no extremes
of fruity pleasures; it's our antidote
to treacherous chatter, our dimeter,
this masquerade of teasing love-note,
where two quake on a crater's perimeter.
What insurance company sets its carriage
by the obfuscations of love or marriage?

XXX

Memory is a funny thing. Oaths sworn
in one generation tossed in the next.
I saw the grief in your eyes when they took away
our silks and red cloth. Forgive me
if I do business with your enemy.
God rushed me in the street and yelled to me:
'Who'll weep for your soul when you're dead?'
The slide of memory isn't benign,
but to change the course of the sun?
Love is still the holy dream. Eastwards,
westwards we scatter like bees lost
for a queen, drunk on light and promise.
The centuries of blood hide their truths well.
Caring for souls is a nasty business.

XXXI

I'd like to write a poem in which guru
was in the first or second line. Then
I'd quote from an Indian sage, pepper
the poetry with references to love,
add a further reference to a spicy affair,
hope the mix was right to salt a wound.
Cinnamon opens the heart. Avoid cumin
if you're in a courting mood. Matchbrokers
know this. A bride must serve papadums
fried in sesame oil if she's to woo a lover.
The bond's snapped, what's left to pick over?
I won't anoint myself with turmeric
or saffron powder. There'll be no garland.
I'll fry some sweets then dip them in syrup.

XXXII

Outside my window the trees shake their leaves
in tremulous anger. The myna bird cannot survive
this gaping anxiety of the leaf in tension
with the wind. My love lies across a sea that smashes
into blue rocks wearied at the sight of lovers:
the men and women lolling in the hard shade,
blunt to the horror of the eroded imagination.
The mind resists. No, this love will last no more
than a season in hell. 'A myth,' you said. 'A myth.'
The gulls in the crevice of the languishing wind
hold their wings aloft in a balancing act only
the watching aerialist perfects. Under the shade
of a casuarina a man gazes at the front of a fire
fanned by the whirling eddy of a northerly.

XXXIII

Your back is broken. It is a ridge of
joints whose dry, synovial fluid leaves
bone on bone to crack osteoporotic.
I will not run my nail across this cracked
pathway of love. My compassion lies
in other directions. I will let loose
the dog of your pain. Do not follow it
into the dark park beyond the road
opposite my house. The ghosts of dead
lovers lurk there, assassins all. Please
proceed to the ready shore by way
of the canal dredged by hard labour.
There you will discover the blue pain
of the people who lived here before us.

XXXIV

The sea is blue today. The saltbush
grey as your love. Sea rushes to shore.
Sea rush spikes upward. The saltmarsh
spreads in all directions. Only cushion bush
keeps tight knots of space. A magpie
looks as if it squats to shit. Only humans
pick up after a dog's poo. The canine
species is doing well in evolutionary speak.

When summer comes the gun sea of metal days
that put me in harm of love's way breaks at your shore.
Stand and wait. There's an empty bottle bobbing
that way. The albatrosses and the seagulls got
to it first: uncorked it and swilled all its medicine.
On your shore the sea is the coolest shade of mock heroic.

XXXV

The tides of your undulating welcome
recall how each season the red-necked
stint, that miracle, traces lines of departure
and arrival. Who will portray its drab beauty,
size, or ancient flyway? Small wings beat fast.
The eastern curlew forages for shrimps,
crabs and worms along the shoreline. No one
knows the secret byways of its return journey.
Between migrations sanderlings dart in and out
of waves, looking for crustaceans, molluscs,
sea worms. Nature is sweet. I am like the hooded
plover. I do not migrate, the trick being
I never have to wait for a quiet gale.

XXXVI

Why do you shadow me? Your shadow
speaks to mine. It tells the things you won't—
like the last time you uttered a cry or prayed.
I don't mind your absence. I endure your loss.
Where you travel there is only silence.
Bring out your lyre. Compose a song of praise.
Let your voice be heard. I can't write songs
for a voice I don't hear. This silence reaches far.
Everything seems dead. The trees seem dead.
They have shed their pain. Hello, Spring!
I dance alone. I throw up my hands, ecstatic.
The blue light of dawn shifts into the grey
of morning. The first silence of the day
begins its tonal play. Behold: Winter!

XXXVII

Our love has the luminescence of a happening elsewhere
we estimate the possible by the angle of the planets
this is all a collective hallucination and a common delusion
everything is given birth in the long hour of the love poem
the delirium of love continues in the age of the self-help book
the surprise is that anyone can believe in anything at all
love punctures itself at the exact moment of our exhaustion
paris is still the city of love but it feels like we're in an ad
we get our take on how to do it right from über-humans
love is unwarranted optimism and proper misunderstanding
it is a heresy to speak of the unnecessary waste of energy
we possess the know-how to engineer our collective rescue
the experience of freedom is the most complete destiny
appalled, we see that everything has already betrayed us

XXXVIII

The sound of your name, like the echo of birds,
hovers in the honeyed space between eternity
and this instant. I nest in arms too strong
for this slight love, night floodlit by dying stars.
The shimmering breath of Scheherazade
floats across the contracting room, a charm
to wear around the neck, like a spell, the crazy
word that will keep you entranced, or not.
I drink the wine of your kisses as if hemlock,
the symphony of death plays its final tune—
before there's nothing and afterwards
the world fades with the sweetest call.
Fragments survive, echoes of sound, but
the exploding world must forget or perish.

XXXIX

The day glides away from me. 'Hello
beautiful lady. I'm just touching base.
Love & peace.' But you breathe
cold into my cells. You send me portraits
of your lonely self: first in Greece
then Egypt. You do not see
the shadow that falls across it. Then
my friend the journalist tells me
that port cities are a man's most fulfilling
dream: the gorgeous girls line up
for their venture with love. In Egypt
I saw the moon drop into the Nile.
That is the portrait I behold.
The desert burnt my hands.

XL

Our bones and ashes carry the words
that holy men, accustomed to love's cancer,
put to music or poetry when in temper.
I gather-in the silence that haunts the seas.
I am a keen hearer of the birdsong
that breaks along those shores
you travel to, away from pain or impulse.
Our bodies carry traces of our fierceness,
cells split into the cancers drugs can't cure.
To kiss the mouth of your acetone love
is the shape of this love's trajectory.
The model is the do-it-yourself manual.
At the edges hover the ghosts of morning.
They know even bland words seduce lovers.

XLI

Spotted dove lands on roof antenna
preferring counterfeit ledge to trees,
which look bare as their geometric
lines soar before window, sapphire
skies coercing colour out of eyes.
A raven balances on bare branch,
grips bare bough verdant with promise,
bark, grown papery to touch, sheds strips.
A helicopter hovers, stuns
starlings to rooftop in fluttery flight.
Cockies zoom into view, their discordant
rhapsodies turning day surreal.
A boy lugs over stone a small plastic seal.
The injury is ecological.

XLII

It is forever news when we drop into love,
and dry as yesterday's dough. Fill up
this jug with the amethyst liquid
of wild vines civilised in vineyards. My bones
lie in subterranean bliss. They are wet
with the moisture of the earth, which revolves
around the sun in an elliptical dream.
Light is the weight of summer. In 8.3
minutes the next ray of light reaches us.
The moon is a luminous object passing off
the bright light of the sun as its own.
A planet is a heavenly body. Venus,
like all the planets, orbits the sun.
Its surface temperature is 460 Celsius.

XLIII

The colour of your name fades in the setting sun.
I'm not indifferent to your passing or travails,
but I can't imagine that the wind brings a new note
or that a fierce gust will turn the sea red.
I will not play the dirge that suits a passing.
Do not ask me to hear the notes that quietened
the screeching of the playful cockatoo or led
your neighbour to marvel what magician
was marooned on his tiny island in the middle
of the green ocean too south for the rescue ships.
The mandolin was my favourite instrument.
You played the notes of my name one by one,
which were resonant and ripe with the season.
My face feels the smack of an unexpected squall.

XLIV

The gull's plaintive cry, high-pitched,
upset me above the din. To be frank,
I felt unsympathetic when I cocked
an ear. The gull had a monotone weep.
It knew only one note. What gall!
I expected when the sea receded,
the tide being far out this daybreak,
its brother gulls, squalling over pickings,
would be directors of my view.
Instead, I saw a pelican amble ashore,
one deep, dragged eye cocked towards eternity,
but the wind picked up and gunmetal seas
pounded the shore. I spun, dazed: Oh, to glide
out of view like the wandering albatross.

XLV

Wave after wave of heat. Where is the cool?
These four hot nights of summer melt
under the armpit. Nothing, no, nothing
matches hell like the pyre inside.
The threatening firestorm arrives,
sucking air from constricted lungs,
the wind howls, as if on heat,
and hot air boils the edge of the sea.
I shrink from touch, as do others, troubled
that our skin, our burning hands, will mould
into unexpected contours, graft alien
selves onto melted intelligence.
On the sly we pose the moral question.

XLVI

I am a skygazer. I am witness to your
eclipse. The blue glow of your beauty
beatifies heaven. I gather myself
around me in horror. In the old temple
love-astrologers hand out business cards.
They spy you parachuting into Mongolia.
How you blacken the sun! It burns with a fiery rim.
This is the time of fear. It grows cold.

The moon bites the sun. Oh the crowd jeers!
It masks the sun. Oh the mob roars! Oh how
people rear their heads like the huge cobra!
In the glow of the dark Venus shone again
on the fallen stones and collapsed columns
of the ancient temples and on the eroded rocks.

XLVII

Waders linger at shoreline for a late
current, a caress of air across wings.
North lie the breeding grounds where chicks scrimmage
in the long day of the tundra summer.
Mudflats give rich pickings before the flight.
Plumage changes into the breeding colours
of tundra pairings, the grey hues
of southern hemisphere no coating
for the sacred matings in the thaw
of marshes, lakes, bogs, icy streams and pools
when surface glaze of permafrost has melted.
Waders rest at staging posts, their ancient
feeding grounds encroached upon by humans.
Mines, rigs, towns and roads engulf the tundra.

XLVIII

I compose my song to the old melody,
swallow the vowels of discordance.
I thought our season of love was over—
it's easy to slip; the unsteady tremble.
An acupuncturist, you needle the memory:
yes, to the old melancholy.
I lose the rhythm, bop a pantomime,
the music grows louder inside my head.
Mind closes to love that's turned absurd—
the song you write a score of litanies,
the verses numbered and squared off.
In tonal dreams your voice resounds
like the old accusations of disharmony
when love burst like a paint bomb.

XLIX

My lover is shitty-eyed,
staying the course because he has to, not coz he wants to.
He is an unlikely pianist who tinkles
the white keys nicely at home when he plays for two, but not here.
He will not sit with my friends, whom he calls amoral,
so he sits alone relishing his principles. Now he's forlorn
and a hypocrite, enjoying surreptitiously
the wobbles of the waitress's sallow breasts.
He turns expectant at the sound of girls atwitter,
mistaking chirps for silly praise or notice,
then swivels round and says I mustn't change the tone,
the organ is *very* orchestral.
My need is for more complex rhythms,
not these irrational utterings of his distress.

L

I thirst. I hunger. This grief is long.
The empty picture-frame glistens.
I collect the letters of your name, like petals,
embalm them in honey, then seal the pot.
The sharp relief of winter never arrives.
This journey is long. I've made a mistake.
Out on the bay the sea whips a windsurfer.
I recall the night of your long pain. I tired early.
I tidy the garden. Tomorrow
I will scoop up the fallen narratives,
like so many fragments never
again assembled or reglued.
The child peeks over the horizon.
Will it be the same story? The same death?

LI

Your words, liquid gold, transform my song,
the sound of your voice as mellifluous
as a bee's humming death conjuring my own,
its sound lost in deserts of reproach.
The room is full of the eyes of those that would
gouge yours. I know the truth of what aches
in your past like my own rushing need
to climb the mountain that frees me from life.
The landscape I see before me is the one
the bones of my ancestors know too well,
but I, like a traitor, move towards yours,
where the pulse of your love charms.
My voice, silent as the wind that steals
through the crack, steadies at last.

LII

This is the music I write. I will not sing it.
The notes are in a key I do not wish to hear.
It is the music of the harrowing road.
I will not speak from inside this madness.
The sound of birds announcing the day
is another reminder that the road
which winds past my house will never
bring tidings of you in spring or summer.
Oh, it's a long time since I had glad tidings.
Love is bought from a man in a yellow suit
selling daisies outside the house
I rented in the land of the distant moon
that nightly swells above my window.
I am weary for summer's sallow promise.

LIII

I want to consume you. Rub your callused
skin with oil from the Sunday markets. I
long for the deep pull of your eyes in the crowd.
I wish a thousand nights of kisses to undo
all memories of your last great love. Without
words to describe the colour of my love—
deep as the emerald I covet in the jeweller's window—
I am helpless to offer reparation. I feel
the pulse of your breath as quick on my skin
as the fevered pulsations of a dying man.
I will take however many steps to find you.
Your back may be broken by the years
of labour in the camps of the abandoned.
When you feel my breath you will embrace me.

LIV

The purple light of fire diminishes,
but nothing checks desire
that pushes against surface and rips reefs.
A gull, shrieking, takes to air.
The green epiphanies of mountains,
dotted with the yellow of lapsed dreams,
bear the mark of light-filled aeons
that suffered the shutter burst of blasphemes.
Churlish guests, like children, insist
on speaking the lassoed word that flying
past becomes the whisper, fragment or gist
that ripens into seas of longing.
The burden is terrible, but borne
for the breathless promise of the hour.

LV

It is the unthinkable that berates me. What if,
what if I were to tell you that it's the long
hour of the night ticking away like a dying
sun that bothers me. What if, what if I were to tell you
that it's not the emptiness looming over life
like disbanding birds that troubles me. What if
I were to tell you that it's not the loss
of your love that worries me. What if I were to tell you
that it's not the thought of your being that occupies me,
but that in the long hour of the night, when all the hours
tick away like a memento of what might have been,
another universe, another try at the impossible, what if
I were to tell you that at that moment it's the impossibility
of our being which troubles me more than our love.

LVI

In the half-light your face performs magic.
Bracing myself I steal from hoary night
what, majestic, belongs to marble repose.
Bittersweet lips angle me in sharp relief.
I'll gorge on ripe berries, pears, to hear again
your madrigal's high notes in cobalt blue.
My music's no match for your melos:
yet in mid-note I turn magpie,
carolling my love, this grubby self,
before an audience gagging with laughter.
What's right for love carved out of ethereal air?
We count nerve cells. Measure the minutes.
Give me what's mine or a reprieve, life.
These shifts in mood are impossible to endure.

LVII

What if I were to tell you that I grabbed
on to the universe, floated out
into the stream of life that connects me,
not to you but to what might yet be, the life led
not as a woman or a man, but as pure thought,
pure light. What if I were to tell you
that we arrived too late for all that might be.
What if I were to tell you that it's the lack
of a compass in my life that makes me
cling to you like driftwood. What if I were
to tell you of my birth into the hour that speaks
of my losses like a blooming flower. What if
I were to tell you that the world opened itself to me
and I saw in its shadows that this goes on forever?

LVIII

I'm back where I vowed I'd not return,
decision once made unmade as if time
unfurled, as if gorgeous beings, imitating
my dance, intend my imitation of them.
The wind that blows away the dust of hope
takes a night's loss for a sign—a reformed gambler,
I'm still gambling on signs, as if the gods
might yet sprinkle blessings and bounty over me,
as if they mean constricted trust to erupt
into a kaleidoscope of second chances.
The gods are cruel. They have an ill-humour.
Let me sleep in sea's crooked arm, a starfish.
Let me gape at far mountains,
at sea routes that flow across my vision.

Printed in Australia
Ingram Content Group Australia Pty Ltd
AUHW021430261124
403343AU00003B/40

9 781925 333626